Quilted Coast

You'll love these 48 great coaster designs to make for family and friends.
Techniques used include machine- and hand-appliqué, piecing and paper-piecing.

By Sue Harvey

General Instructions

The coaster sets are divided into four coasters per set. In the set are four different designs. Construction methods vary—machine appliqué, hand appliqué, pieced (either by machine or by hand) and paper-pieced. Rather than repeat basic construction instructions for each set, the following general instructions are given. Refer back to this section as you create your coaster sets.

Machine Appliqué

1. Sew ¾" x 4½" border strips to two opposite sides of the background fabric; press. Sew ¾" x 5" border strips to two remaining sides to form coaster top as shown in Figure 1; press.

2. Place coaster top right sides together with backing fabric; place a batting square under backing fabric as shown in Figure 2.

3. Sew around edge using a ¼" seam allowance; leave a 2" opening on one side. Turn right side out; hand-stitch opening closed.

4. Bond fusible transfer web to wrong side of fabric scraps to be used for appliqué following manufacturer's instructions.

5. Make a paper or plastic pattern for each piece to be appliquéd using pattern pieces given with pattern. Place patterns facedown on appropriate fabric scraps; trace and cut out each piece. Remove paper backing.

6. Place each piece on background fabric in the order indicated on the pattern pieces; fuse in place.

7. Satin-stitch around each shape using a coordinating thread in the top of the machine and thread to match the coaster backing in the bobbin.

Hand Appliqué

1. Sew ¾" x 4½" border strips to two opposite sides of background fabric; press. Sew ¾" x 5" border strips to the two remaining sides to form coaster top as shown in Figure 1; press.

2. Cut out each piece to be appliquéd adding a ⅛" to ¼" seam allowance. Turn under seam allowance after cutting.

3. Appliqué pieces in place on background fabric in the order shown on pattern pieces.

4. Place coaster top right sides together with backing fabric; place a batting square under backing fabric as shown in Figure 2.

5. Sew around the edge using a ¼" seam allowance; leave a 2" opening on one side. Turn right side out; hand-stitch opening closed.

6. Hand- or machine-quilt as desired.

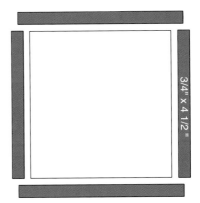

Figure 1
Sew border strips to background square to form coaster top.

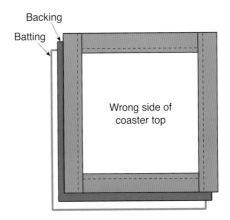

Figure 2
Place coaster top and backing right sides together; place batting under backing.

Pieced

1. Prepare templates using pattern pieces given. Cut pieces as indicated for each coaster. Cut border strips, backing and batting pieces as indicated for each coaster set.

2. Follow Block Piecing Diagrams for each pieced coaster.

3. Sew ¾" x 4½" border strips to two opposite sides of pieced coaster; press. Sew ¾" x 5" border strips to the two remaining sides to form the coaster top as shown in Figure 1; press.

4. Place coaster top right sides together with backing fabric; place a batting square under backing fabric as shown in Figure 2.

5. Sew around edge using a ¼" seam allowance; leave a 2" opening on one side. Turn right side out; hand-stitch opening closed.

6. Hand- or machine-quilt as desired.

Paper-Pieced

1. Copy or trace the full-size paper-piecing patterns for each coaster. *Note: Fabric pieces will be placed on the front of the pattern; sewing will be done on the back of the pattern. If pattern lines are not visible on the back, trace lines on the back also.*

2. Cut a scrap of fabric at least ¼" larger on all sides than each area. Place fabric over area 1 on pattern front. Place area 2 fabric right sides together over area 1 fabric. Set machine for 14-18 stitches per inch. Stitch on pattern back along the line between areas 1 and 2 beginning one stitch before line and ending one stitch beyond line.

3. Trim seam allowance. Fold fabric 2 over area 2 on the pattern; press seam open.

4. Continue to add pieces following the numerical order and fabric colors on pattern to complete each block section. *Note: Some blocks are pieced in sections. Sew block sections together to form completed block.*

5. Trim to the outside of block seam allowance. Leave paper pattern intact.

6. Cut backing and batting pieces as indicated for each coaster set.

7. Place pieced coaster top right sides together with a backing piece; place a batting piece under backing piece as shown in Figure 2.

8. Sew around edge along sewing line; leave a 2" opening on one side.

9. Remove paper pattern. Turn right side out. Hand-stitch opening closed.

10. Hand- or machine-quilt as desired. ●

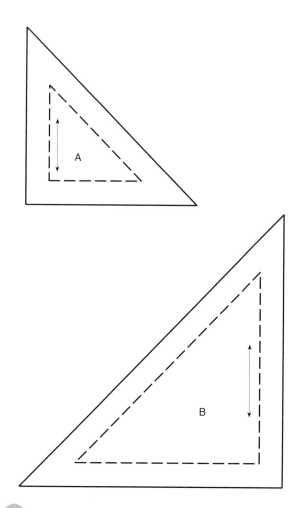

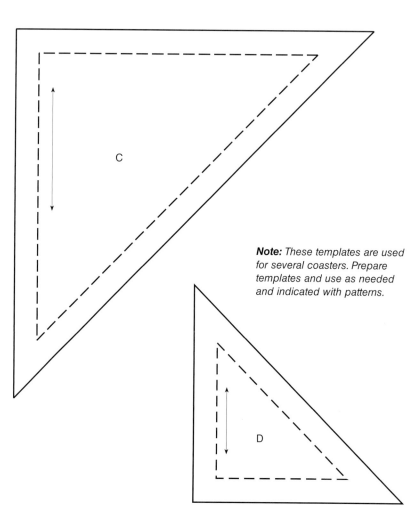

Note: These templates are used for several coasters. Prepare templates and use as needed and indicated with patterns.

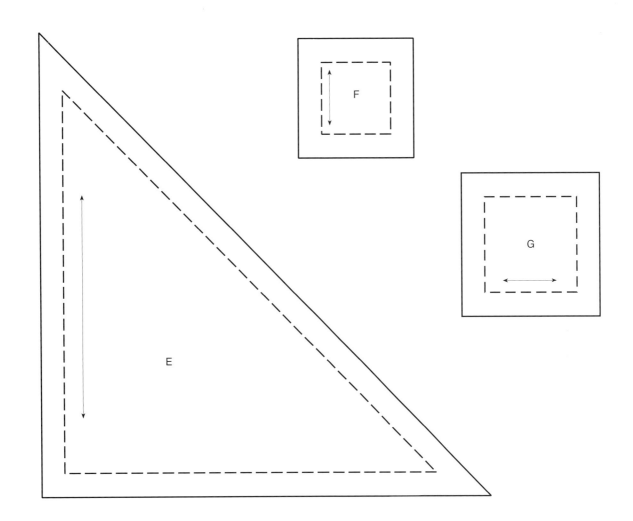

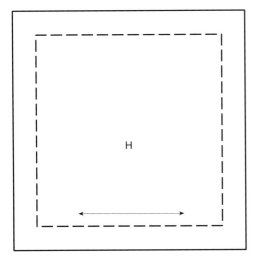

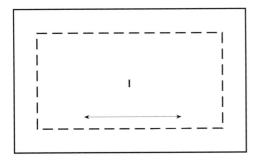

Meet the Designer

Sue Harvey has been involved with a variety of crafts ranging from basketmaking to folk-art painting for more than 15 years. When she took her first quilting class in 1989, she put away all those other supplies and has been designing and making quilts ever since.

She has been an active member of the Schoolhouse Quilters Guild for five years, serving as their president for three years. She is also a member of the Pine Tree Quilters Guild.

Sue is an avid gardener. She says, "Gardening is like quilting except you use plants and flowers instead of fabric to make beautiful patchwork." She has been a Master Gardener for three years. Torn between these two passions, she has taught an appliqué class and an herb gardening class. She has designed quilts for House of White Birches and coordinates the Master Gardener Herb Garden each summer.

She and her husband, Clayton, live in Enfield, Maine, where the weather perfectly complements her activities—cooler winters for quilting and warm summers for gardening.

Heart 'n' Home Coaster Set

These heart-shaped coasters are filled with houses or trees. The colors reflect the country folk-art style prevalent in many home decors. Substitute bright colors or pastels to fit your decorating pleasure.

Heart/House 1 Coaster
Placement Diagram
Approximately 4 1/2" x 5"

Heart/House 2 Coaster
Placement Diagram
Approximately 4 1/2" x 5"

Project Specifications
Coaster Size: 4½" x 5"
Block Size: 2½" x 2½"
Number of Blocks: 4

Materials for the Set
- Scraps cream, rust, black and brown solids; red, dark red, blue, brown, light green, medium green and dark green prints for house and tree blocks
- Assorted scraps for crazy-patch heart border
- 12" x 12" square black solid for backing
- 12" x 12" square batting
- Black all-purpose thread for piecing
- Basic sewing supplies and tools and tracing paper

Cutting Chart for the Set
1. Cut four heart-shaped black solid backing pieces and four heart-shaped batting pieces using paper-pieced heart as template.

Instructions
1. Follow steps 1–5 General Instructions for paper-pieced coasters to complete the house and tree blocks.
2. Copy or trace a full-size heart pattern for each coaster.
3. Place a paper-pieced house block over area 1 of the heart-shaped paper pattern; align outer edge of the house block with the dashed line on the heart pattern.
4. Using this as area 1 fabric, follow steps 2–10 of General Instructions for paper-pieced coasters to complete coaster.
5. Repeat for remaining house block and two tree blocks. ●

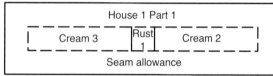

House 1 Part 1 — Cream 3, Rust 1, Cream 2 — Seam allowance

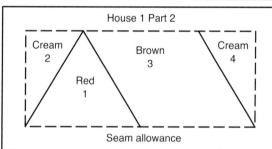

House 1 Part 2 — Cream 2, Red 1, Brown 3, Cream 4 — Seam allowance

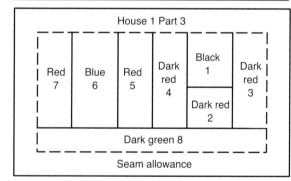

House 1 Part 3 — Red 7, Blue 6, Red 5, Dark red 4, Black 1, Dark red 2, Dark red 3, Dark green 8 — Seam allowance

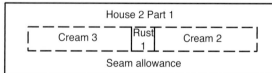

House 2 Part 1 — Cream 3, Rust 1, Cream 2 — Seam allowance

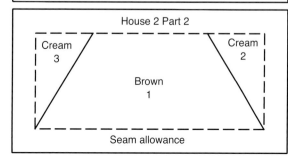

House 2 Part 2 — Cream 3, Brown 1, Cream 2 — Seam allowance

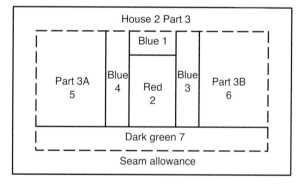

House 2 Part 3 — Part 3A 5, Blue 4, Blue 1, Red 2, Blue 3, Part 3B 6, Dark green 7 — Seam allowance

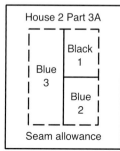

House 2 Part 3A — Blue 3, Black 1, Blue 2 — Seam allowance

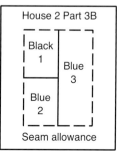

House 2 Part 3B — Black 1, Blue 3, Blue 2 — Seam allowance

4

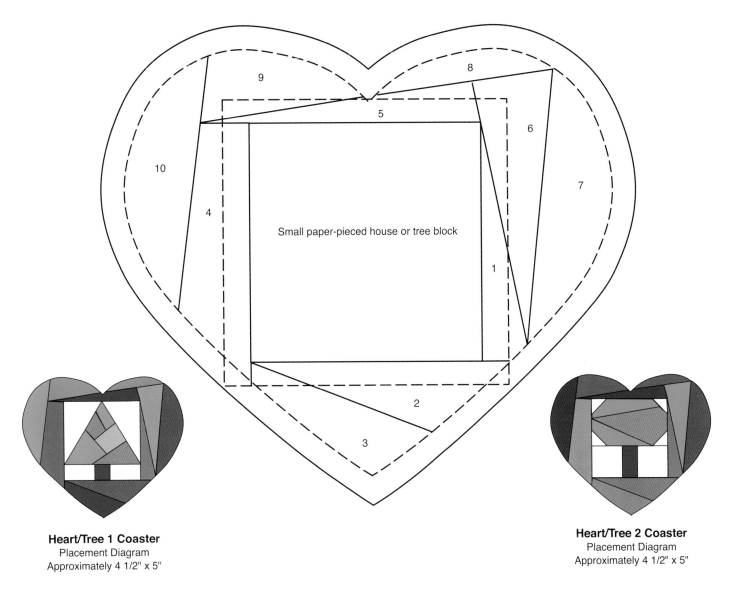

Small paper-pieced house or tree block

9

8

5

6

10

4

1

7

2

3

Heart/Tree 1 Coaster
Placement Diagram
Approximately 4 1/2" x 5"

Heart/Tree 2 Coaster
Placement Diagram
Approximately 4 1/2" x 5"

Tree 1 Part 1

Cream
7

1
Light
green

2

Cream
6

Medium
green

3

4

Medium green

Dark green

5

Dark green

Seam allowance

Tree 2 Part 1

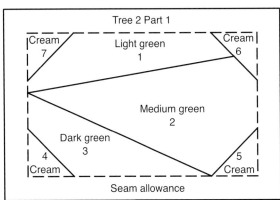

Cream
7

Light green
1

Cream
6

Medium green
2

Dark green
3

4
Cream

5
Cream

Seam allowance

Tree 1 Part 2

Cream
3

Brown
1

Cream
2

Seam allowance

Tree 2 Part 2

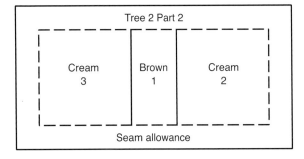

Cream
3

Brown
1

Cream
2

Seam allowance

Grandmother's Favorites Coaster Set

Classic quilt designs from Grandmother's era are well known to everyone—
Sunbonnet Sue, Grandmother's Flower Garden, Dresden Plate and Grandmother's Fan.
Try making miniature versions of these old favorites for this coaster set.

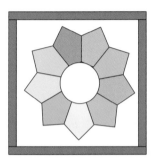

Dresden Plate Coaster
Placement Diagram
4 1/2" x 4 1/2"

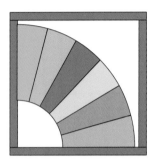

Fan Coaster
Placement Diagram
4 1/2" x 4 1/2"

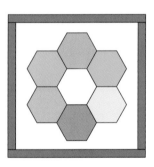

Flower Garden Coaster
Placement Diagram
4 1/2" x 4 1/2"

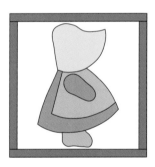

Sunbonnet Sue Coaster
Placement Diagram
4 1/2" x 4 1/2"

Project Specifications

Coaster Size: 4½" x 4½"
Block Size: 4" x 4"
Number of Blocks: 4

Materials for the Set

- 10" x 10" square white floral print for background
- Scraps peach, purple, blue, pink, turquoise, yellow, green and teal 1930s reproduction prints
- Fat quarter blue solid for backing and borders
- 10" x 10" square batting
- 10" x 10" piece fusible transfer web
- White and blue all-purpose thread
- Basic sewing supplies and tools

Cutting Chart for the Set

1. Cut four squares white floral print 4½" x 4½" for background.
2. Cut four squares blue solid 5" x 5" for backing.
3. Cut four squares batting 5" x 5".
4. Cut eight strips blue solid ¾" x 4½" for borders.
5. Cut eight strips blue solid ¾" x 5" for borders.

Instructions

1. Follow General Instructions and Special Instructions given for each set.
2. Satin-stitch each coaster with white thread in the top of the machine and blue thread in the bobbin.

Dresden Plate Special Instructions

1. Follow steps 1–3 of General Instructions for Machine Appliqué.
2. Cut pieces as directed on template. Sew plate units together as shown in Figure 1.

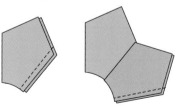

Figure 1
Sew plate units together as shown.

3. Carefully fuse web to the back of the pieced plate shape. Peel off paper backing. Trim away any web-bing extending beyond edges or into center of plate.

4. Position plate shape on the prepared coaster top; cover with pressing cloth and fuse in place.

5. Satin-stitch in place.

Flower Garden Special Instructions

1. Follow steps 1–3 of the General Instructions for Machine Appliqué.

2. Cut pieces as directed on template.

3. Sew hexagons together to form large flower as shown in Figure 2; press.

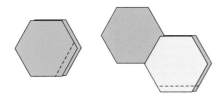

Figure 2
Sew hexagon units together as shown.

4. Carefully fuse web to the back of the pieced flower shape. Peel off paper backing. Trim away any web-bing extending beyond edges of flower.

5. Position pieced shape on prepared coaster top; cover with pressing cloth and fuse in place.

6. Satin-stitch in place.

Fan Special Instructions

1. Cut pieces as directed on template.

2. Sew fan blades together as shown in Figure 3.

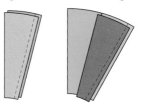

Figure 3
Sew fan blades together as shown.

3. Carefully fuse web to the back of the pieced fan shape. Peel off paper backing. Trim away any web-bing extending beyond edges of fan.

4. Position pieced fan shape on 4½" x 4½" white floral background square; cover with pressing cloth and fuse in place.

5. Follow steps 1–3 of General Instructions for Machine Appliqué.

6. Satin-stitch in place. ●

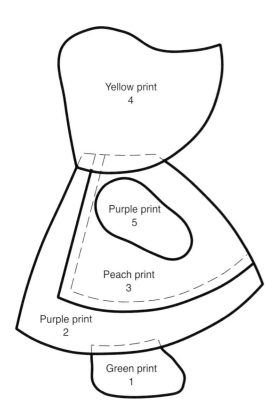

Yellow print
4

Purple print
5

Peach print
3

Purple print
2

Green print
1

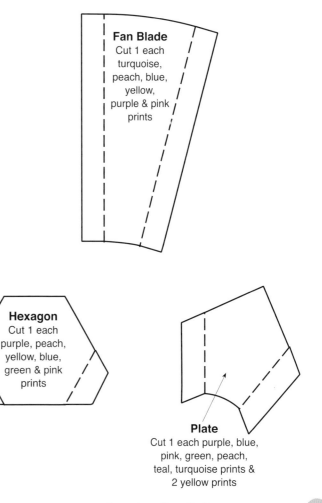

Fan Blade
Cut 1 each turquoise, peach, blue, yellow, purple & pink prints

Hexagon
Cut 1 each purple, peach, yellow, blue, green & pink prints

Plate
Cut 1 each purple, blue, pink, green, peach, teal, turquoise prints & 2 yellow prints

Star Shine Coaster Set

*Four different star designs are used to create this bright yellow,
blue and white coaster set which can be either hand- or machine-pieced.*

Project Specifications

Coaster Size: 4½" x 4½"
Block Size: 4" x 4"
Number of Blocks: 4

Materials for the Set

- Fat quarter blue print
- 10" x 10" square each yellow and white/black prints
- 10" x 10" square batting
- Blue all-purpose thread
- Basic sewing supplies and tools

Cutting Chart for the Set

1. Cut four squares batting 5" x 5" and four squares blue print 5" x 5" for backing.
2. Cut eight strips each blue print ¾" x 4½" and ¾" x 5" for borders.

Instructions

1. Follow General Instructions for Pieced Coaster to complete the set. ●

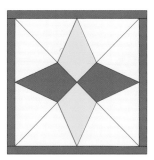

Connecting Star Coaster
Placement Diagram
4 1/2" x 4 1/2"

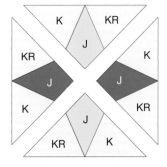

Connecting Star
Block Piecing Diagram
Lay out pieces to complete
1 Connecting Star block.

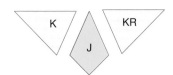

Connecting Star Units
Make 4 units.

Connecting Star Template Cutting Chart

J—Cut 2 yellow print & 2 blue print

K—Cut 8 white/black print; (reverse half for KR)

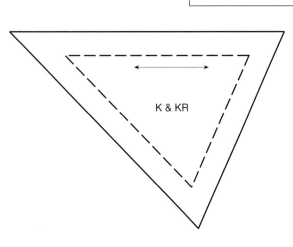

K & KR

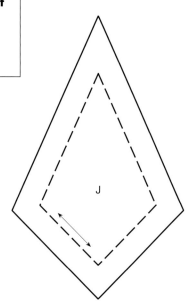

J

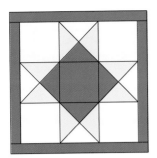

Ohio Star Coaster
Placement Diagram
4 1/2" x 4 1/2"

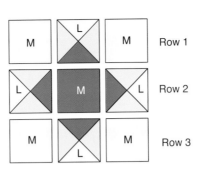

Row 1

Row 2

Row 3

Ohio Star
Block Piecing Diagram
Lay out pieces to complete 1 Ohio Star block.

Ohio Star Units
Combine triangles as above to form
4 squares for Ohio Star block.

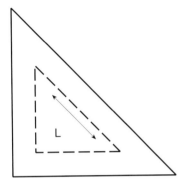

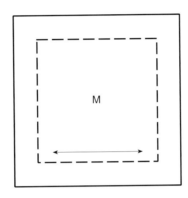

Ohio Star Template Cutting Chart

L—Cut 8 yellow print & 4 each white/black
& blue prints

M—Cut 4 white/black print & 1 blue print

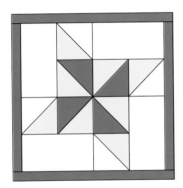

Spinning Star Coaster
Placement Diagram
4 1/2" x 4 1/2"

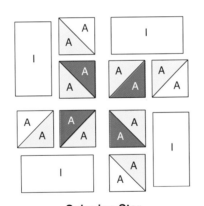

Spinning Star
Block Piecing Diagram
Lay out pieces to complete 1 Spinning Star block.

Spinning Star Units
Make 4 of each unit. Press seams
toward yellow A in the yellow/white
units; press seams toward the blue A in
the yellow/blue units.

Spinning Star Template Cutting Chart

A—Cut 8 yellow print & 4 each white/black &
blue prints

I—Cut 4 white/black prints

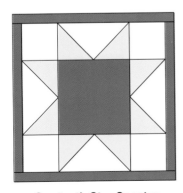

Sawtooth Star Coaster
Placement Diagram
4 1/2" x 4 1/2"

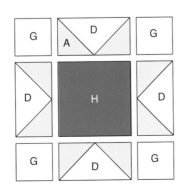

Sawtooth Star
Block Piecing Diagram
Lay out pieces to complete 1 Sawtooth
Star block.

Sawtooth Star Units
Make 4 units.

Sawtooth Star Template Cutting Chart

A—Cut 8 yellow print

D—Cut 4 white/black print

G—Cut 4 white/black print

H—Cut 1 blue print

Merry Christmas Coaster Set

Entertaining is a major part of the Christmas season. Make a set of these coasters as practical decorative accents around your home or make them into Christmas ornaments by adding a hanging string to one corner.

Project Specifications

Coaster Size: 4½" x 4½"
Block Size: 4" x 4"
Number of Blocks: 4

Materials for the Set

- 10" x 10" square tan print for background
- Scraps green print #1, green print #2, red plaid #1, red plaid #2; brown, gold and red prints; and black, peach, red and white solids for appliqué
- Scraps white felt for appliqué
- Fat quarter green/red print for backing and borders
- 10" x 10" square batting
- 10" x 10" piece fusible transfer web
- All-purpose thread to match appliqué fabrics
- 1 spool green all-purpose thread to match backing
- Gold all-purpose thread
- Permanent black fabric pen
- Basic sewing supplies and tools

Cutting Chart for the Set

1. Cut four squares tan print 4½" x 4½" for background.
2. Cut four squares green/red print 5" x 5" for backing.
3. Cut four squares batting 5" x 5".
4. Cut eight strips green/red print ¾" x 4½" for borders.
5. Cut eight strips green/red print ¾" x 5" for borders.

Instructions

1. Follow General Instructions for Machine Appliqué and Special Instructions noted with individual patterns to complete this set.

Santa Special Instructions

1. Cut coat as one large piece.
2. Make dots for eyes using permanent black fabric pen.

Angel Special Instructions

1. Cut wings, dress and arms as one piece each.
2. Make dots for eyes using permanent black fabric pen.
3. Satin-stitch candle flame using gold thread. ●

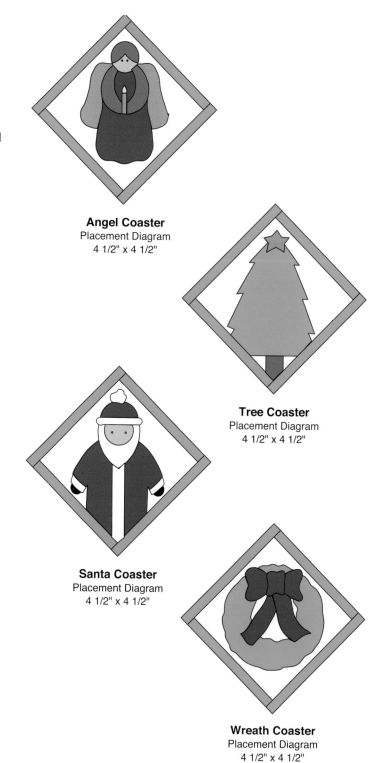

Angel Coaster
Placement Diagram
4 1/2" x 4 1/2"

Tree Coaster
Placement Diagram
4 1/2" x 4 1/2"

Santa Coaster
Placement Diagram
4 1/2" x 4 1/2"

Wreath Coaster
Placement Diagram
4 1/2" x 4 1/2"

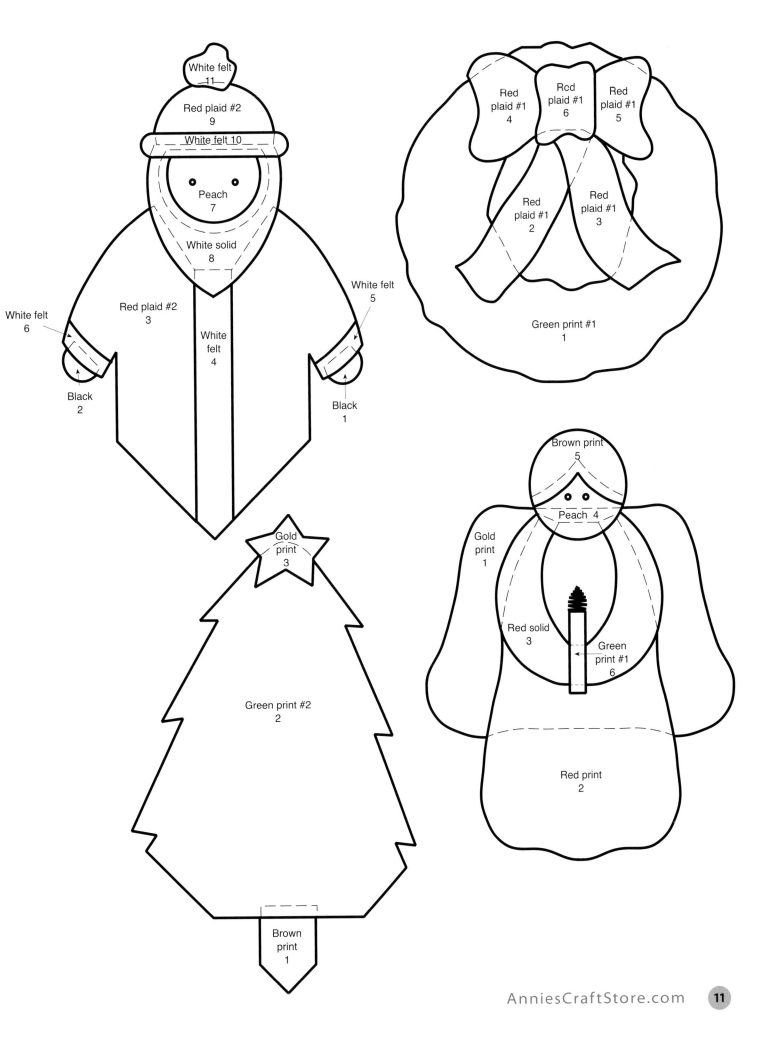

White felt
11

Red plaid #2
9

White felt 10

Peach
7

White solid
8

White felt
5

White felt
6

Red plaid #2
3

White
felt
4

Black
2

Black
1

Red
plaid #1
4

Rcd
plaid #1
6

Red
plaid #1
5

Red
plaid #1
2

Red
plaid #1
3

Green print #1
1

Gold
print
3

Green print #2
2

Brown
print
1

Brown print
5

Peach 4

Gold
print
1

Red solid
3

Green
print #1
6

Red print
2

Basket Case Coaster Set

Basket patterns look good in any size block. These pretty coasters would be the perfect accent for your next tea party.

Project Specifications

Coaster Size: 4½" x 4½"
Block Size: 4" x 4"
Number of Blocks: 4

Materials for the Set

- 12" x 12" square dark green print for backing and borders
- 6" x 6" squares each peach, blue, pink and purple floral prints
- Scraps light peach, dark peach, light blue, dark blue, light pink, dark pink, light purple and dark purple prints
- 10" x 10" square batting
- Cream all-purpose thread for piecing
- Dark green all-purpose thread for finishing
- Basic sewing supplies and tools

Cutting Chart for the Set

1. Cut four squares batting 5" x 5" and four squares dark green print 5" x 5" for backing.

2. Cut eight strips each dark green print ¾" x 4½" and ¾" x 5" for borders.

Instructions

1. Cut pieces for each coaster as indicated in separate cutting charts. *Note: The piece indicated with an * on the Block Piecing Diagrams should be cut carefully to place a flower at its center to give the effect of a flower in each basket.*

2. Hand- or machine-appliqué handle to floral C piece on two of the basket designs.

3. Follow General Instructions for Pieced Coaster to complete the set. ●

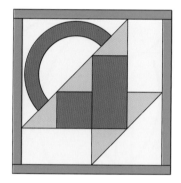

Heart Basket Coaster
Placement Diagram
4 1/2" x 4 1/2"

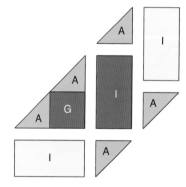

Heart Basket Units
Piece units as shown for Heart Basket block.

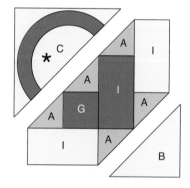

Heart Basket
Block Piecing Diagram
Lay out pieces to complete 1 Heart Basket block. Appliqué handle piece to C before sewing C to the pieced unit.

Heart Basket Template Cutting Chart

A—Cut 5 light pink print

B—Cut 1 pink floral print

C—Cut 1 pink floral print

G—Cut 1 dark pink print

I—Cut 1 dark pink & 2 pink floral print

Handle—Cut 1 dark pink (add ⅛"–¼" seam allowance)

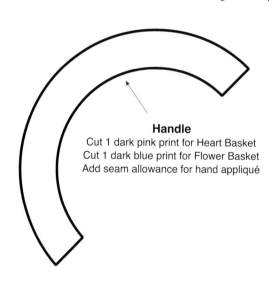

Handle
Cut 1 dark pink print for Heart Basket
Cut 1 dark blue print for Flower Basket
Add seam allowance for hand appliqué

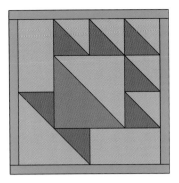

Fruit Basket Coaster
Placement Diagram
4 1/2" x 4 1/2"

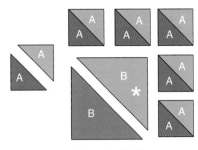

Fruit Basket Units
Piece units as shown.

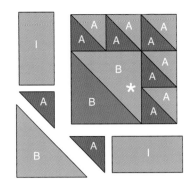

Fruit Basket
Block Piecing Diagram
Lay out pieces to complete 1
Fruit Basket block.

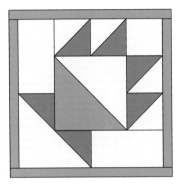

Cactus Basket Coaster
Placement Diagram
4 1/2" x 4 1/2"

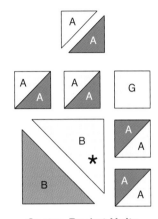

Cactus Basket Units
Piece units as shown.

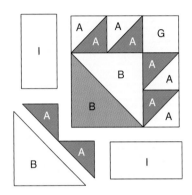

Cactus Basket
Block Piecing Diagram
Lay out pieces to complete 1 Cactus Basket block.

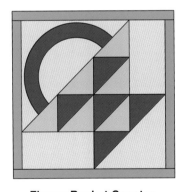

Flower Basket Coaster
Placement Diagram
4 1/2" x 4 1/2"

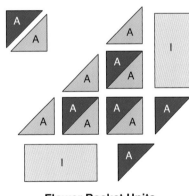

Flower Basket Units
Piece units as shown.

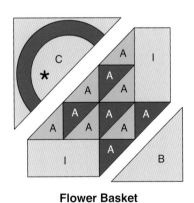

Flower Basket
Block Piecing Diagram
Lay out pieces to complete 1
Flower Basket block. Appliqué
handle piece to C before sewing
C to the pieced unit.

Fruit Basket Template Cutting Chart

A—Cut 5 purple floral print & 7 dark purple print

B—Cut 1 light purple print & 2 purple floral print

I—Cut 2 purple floral print

Cactus Basket Template Cutting Chart

A—Cut 4 peach floral print & 6 dark peach print

B—Cut 1 light peach print & 2 peach floral print

G—Cut 1 peach floral print

I—Cut 2 peach floral print

Flower Basket Template Cutting Chart

A—Cut 5 dark blue & 6 light blue print

B—Cut 1 blue floral print

C—Cut 1 blue floral print

I—Cut 2 blue floral print

Handle—Cut 1 dark blue print (add 1/8"–1/4" seam allowance)

In the Cabin Coaster Set

Try paper piecing these Log Cabin design coasters. Each coaster has a different design. Using Christmas colors makes them perfect holiday gifts or decorative accents.

Project Specifications

Coaster Size: 4 ¼" x 4 ¼"
Block Size: 4 ¼" x 4 ¼"
Number of Blocks: 4

Materials for the Set

- Fat quarter of green print
- 10" x 10" square cream print
- 5" x 5" square burgundy print
- 10" x 10" square batting
- Dark green all-purpose thread
- Basic sewing supplies and tools and tracing paper

Cutting Chart for the Set

1. Cut four squares each green print and batting 4¾" x 4¾".
2. Cut several strips green and cream fabrics 1" by fabric width.
3. Cut four squares burgundy print 1¾" x 1¾" for centers.

Instructions

1. Follow General Instructions for paper-pieced coasters to complete the set. ●

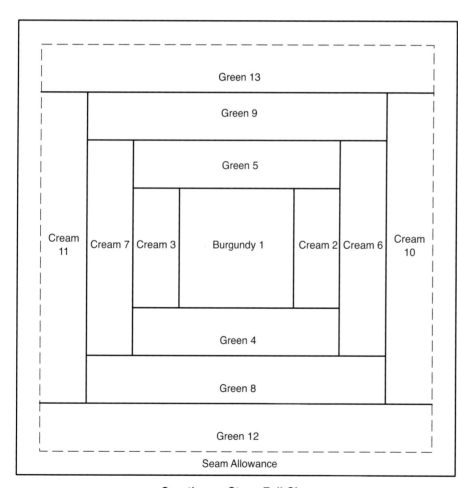

**Courthouse Steps Full-Size
Paper-Piecing Pattern**

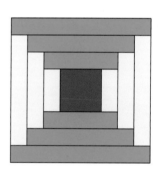

Courthouse Steps Coaster
Placement Diagram
4 1/4" x 4 1/4"

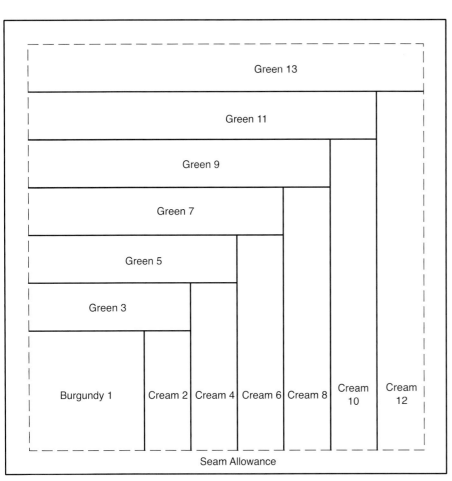

Half-Log Cabin Full-Size Paper-Piecing Pattern

The diagram contains the following labeled pieces:
- Green 13
- Green 11
- Green 9
- Green 7
- Green 5
- Green 3
- Burgundy 1
- Cream 2
- Cream 4
- Cream 6
- Cream 8
- Cream 10
- Cream 12
- Seam Allowance

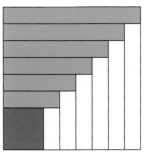

Half Log Cabin Coaster
Placement Diagram
4 1/4" x 4 1/4"

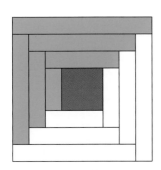

Log Cabin Coaster
Placement Diagram
4 1/4" x 4 1/4"

Log Cabin Full-Size Paper-Piecing Pattern

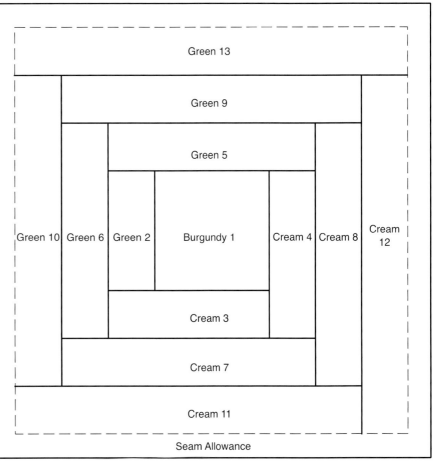

The diagram contains the following labeled pieces:
- Green 13
- Green 9
- Green 5
- Green 10
- Green 6
- Green 2
- Burgundy 1
- Cream 4
- Cream 8
- Cream 12
- Cream 3
- Cream 7
- Cream 11
- Seam Allowance

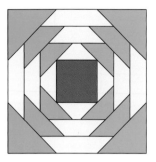

Pineapple Log Cabin Coaster
Placement Diagram
4 1/4" x 4 1/4"

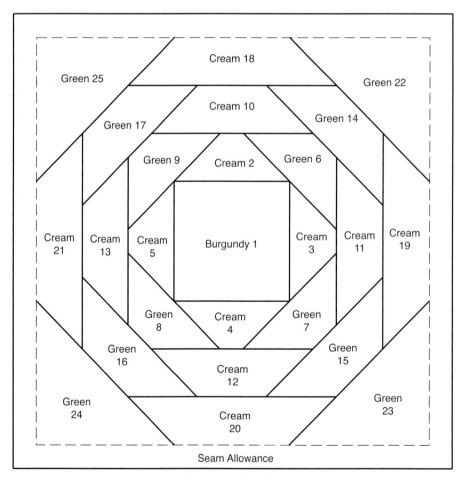

**Pineapple Full-Size
Paper-Piecing Pattern**

Winter Coaster Set

Outdoor activities for winter include sledding, skating and making snowmen. To be warm in the cold, one must wear a hat and mittens. Use these coasters under mugs of cocoa after playing outside.

Project Specifications

Coaster Size: 4½" x 4½"
Block Size: 4" x 4"
Number of Blocks: 4

Materials for the Set

- 10" x 10" square cream solid for background
- Scraps red/black check, red dot, tan, dark brown, gray and blue prints and white solid for appliqué
- Scraps red and white felt for appliqué
- Fat quarter dark blue/light blue print for backing and borders
- 10" x 10" square batting
- 10" x 10" piece fusible transfer web
- All-purpose thread to match appliqué fabrics
- Blue all-purpose thread to match backing
- Black and brown all-purpose thread
- Permanent blue fabric pen
- Basic sewing supplies and tools

Cutting Chart for Set

1. Cut four squares cream solid 4½" x 4½" for background.
2. Cut four squares dark blue/light blue print 5" x 5" for backing.
3. Cut four squares batting 5" x 5".
4. Cut eight strips dark blue/light blue print ¾" x 4½" for borders.
5. Cut eight strips dark blue/light blue print ¾" x 5" for borders.

Instructions

1. Follow General Instructions for Machine Appliqué and Special Instructions noted with individual patterns to complete this set.

Snowman Special Instructions

1. Stitch mouth and eyes using black thread.
2. Stitch twig arms using brown thread.

Skates Special Instructions

1. Stitch skate laces using black thread.

Sled Special Instructions

1. Write the letters on sled using permanent blue fabric pen. ●

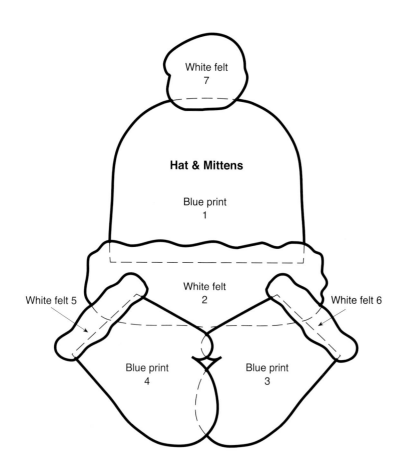

White felt
7

Hat & Mittens

Blue print
1

White felt
2

White felt 5

White felt 6

Blue print
4

Blue print
3

Hat & Mittens Coaster
Placement Diagram
4 1/2" x 4 1/2"

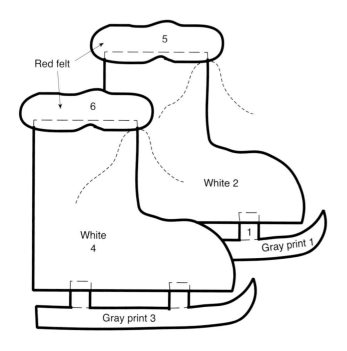

5

Red felt

6

White 2

White
4

1

Gray print 1

Gray print 3

Skates Coaster
Placement Diagram
4 1/2" x 4 1/2"

Snowman Coaster
Placement Diagram
4 1/2" x 4 1/2"

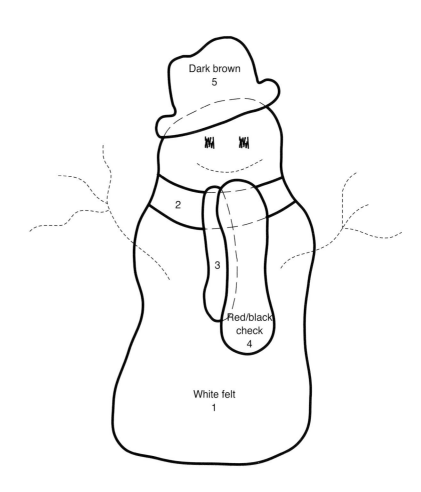

Dark brown
5

2

3

Red/black
check
4

White felt
1

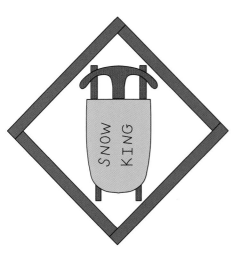

Sled Coaster
Placement Diagram
4 1/2" x 4 1/2"

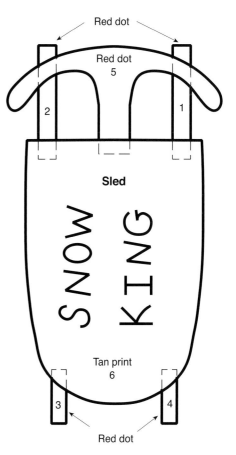

Red dot

Red dot
5

2   1

Sled

SNOW KING

Tan print
6

3   4

Red dot

Spring Coaster Set

Spring brings windy kite-flying days, rainy umbrella days and those days when we catch sight of the first flowers and birds of the season. Celebrate the end of winter by making these coasters that feature spring motifs.

Project Specifications

Coaster Size: 4½" x 4½"
Block Size: 4" x 4"
Number of Blocks: 4

Materials for the Set

- 10" x 10" square cream solid for background
- Scraps medium blue, light blue, yellow, green, light pink, dark pink, tan and light brown prints for appliqué
- Fat quarter floral print for backing and borders
- 10" x 10" square batting
- 10" x 10" piece fusible transfer web
- All-purpose thread to match appliqué fabrics
- All-purpose thread to match backing
- 6-strand pink embroidery floss
- Black, light blue and pink all-purpose thread
- Basic sewing supplies and tools

Cutting Chart for the Set

1. Cut four squares cream solid 4½" x 4½" for background.
2. Cut four squares floral print 5" x 5" for backing.
3. Cut four squares batting 5" x 5".
4. Cut eight strips floral print ¾" x 4½" for borders.
5. Cut eight strips floral print ¾" x 5" for borders.

Instructions

1. Follow General Instructions for Machine Appliqué and Special Instructions noted with individual patterns to complete this set.

Kite Cutting Special Instructions

1. Stitch kite crosspiece and string using black thread.
2. Stitch tail using pink thread.
3. Using 2 strands pink floss, go down through coaster top and back up through coaster; tie a small bow on the kite tail referring to the pattern. Repeat for the second bow.

Umbrella Special Instructions

1. Satin-stitch umbrella tip using black thread.

Bird's Nest Special Instructions

1. Cut inside of nest from wrong side of tan fabric; cut outside of nest from right side of fabric.
2. Cut out eggs as one large piece.
3. Stitch individual egg lines using light blue thread. ●

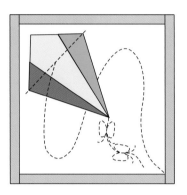

Kite Coaster
Placement Diagram
4 1/2" x 4 1/2"

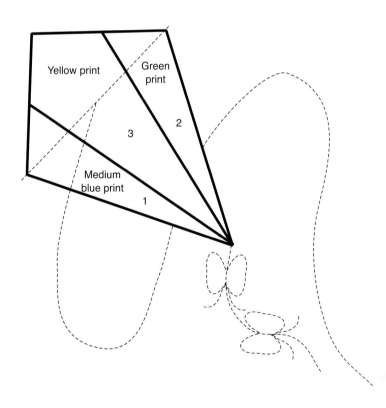

Yellow print

Green print

Medium blue print

2

3

1

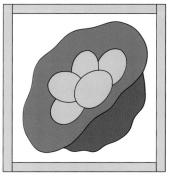

Bird's Nest Coaster
Placement Diagram
4 1/2" x 4 1/2"

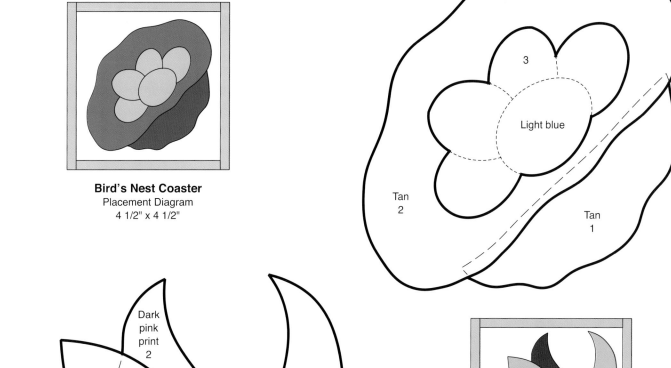

3

Light blue

Tan
2

Tan
1

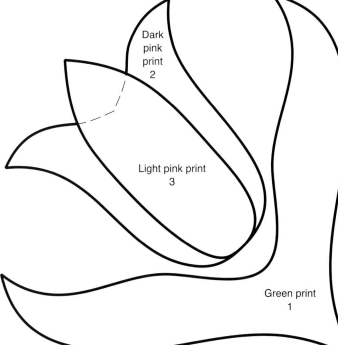

Dark
pink
print
2

Light pink print
3

Green print
1

Tulip Coaster
Placement Diagram
4 1/2" x 4 1/2"

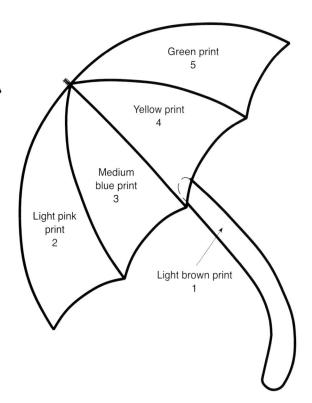

Green print
5

Yellow print
4

Medium
blue print
3

Light pink
print
2

Light brown print
1

Umbrella Coaster
Placement Diagram
4 1/2" x 4 1/2"

Summer Coaster Set

Watermelon, gardening, flowers, sailing—all of these are motifs that remind us of summer. Make a set of coasters for your summer living using these appliqué designs.

Project Specifications

Coaster Size: 4½" x 4½"

Block Size: 4" x 4"

Number of Blocks: 4

Materials for the Set

- 10" x 10" square cream solid for background
- Scraps sunflower print, red solid, blue-and-white check, brown plaid, red/navy stripe; and red, green, gold, navy, red star, navy star and blue prints for appliqué
- Fat quarter red/blue print for backing and borders
- 10" x 10" square batting
- 10" x 10" piece fusible transfer web
- All-purpose thread to match appliqué fabrics
- 1 spool blue all-purpose thread to match backing
- Basic sewing supplies and tools

Cutting Chart for the Set

1. Cut four squares cream solid 4½" x 4½" for background.
2. Cut four squares red/blue print 5" x 5" for backing.
3. Cut four squares batting 5" x 5".
4. Cut eight strips red/blue print ¾" x 4½" for borders.
5. Cut eight strips red/blue print ¾" x 5" for borders.

Instructions

1. Follow General Instructions for Machine Appliqué and Special Instructions noted with individual patterns to complete this set.

Sailboat Special Instructions

1. To make pieced background, mark water-edge line on one 4½" x 4½" cream background square.
2. Draw a line ¼" away from edge line. Cut along this line referring to Figure 1; discard bottom piece. Place right sides together with blue print triangle referring to Figure 2; stitch, leaving a ¼" seam allowance. Press.

Sunflower Special Instructions

1. Place two sunflower petals right sides together; stitch around edge leaving bottom open; turn. Repeat to make eight petals.
2. Place petals on coaster referring to the block drawing; baste in place.

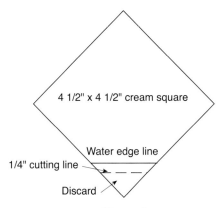

Figure 1
Draw line 1/4" away from edge line; cut along line.

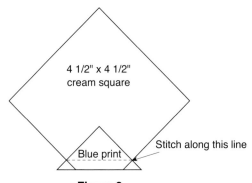

Figure 2
Stitch blue print triangle along line.

3. Cut a piece of fusible transfer web 3" x 3". Fuse to a scrap of brown plaid. Trace circle for sunflower center on paper side of fusible transfer web. Cut out circle, remove paper backing and fuse in place over petals.
4. Satin-stitch around edge of circle, catching bottom of petals and leaving tips free.

Watermelon Special Instructions

1. Cut out green watermelon as one piece.
2. To make pieced background, mark tablecloth edge line on one 4½" x 4½" cream background square.

3. Draw a line ¼" away from this line referring to Figure 3; cut along this line.

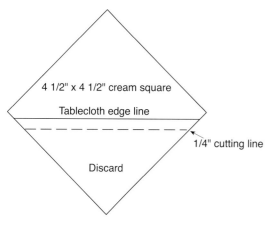

Figure 3
Draw line 1/4" away
from edge line.

4. Place right sides together with blue-and-white check triangle and stitch referring to Figure 4. ●

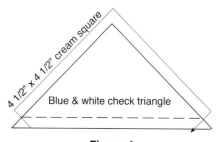

Figure 4
Sew blue-and-white check triangle along line.

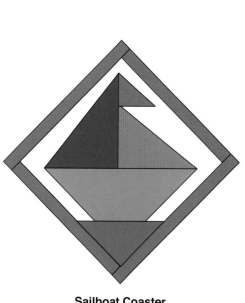

Sailboat Coaster
Placement Diagram
4 1/2" x 4 1/2"

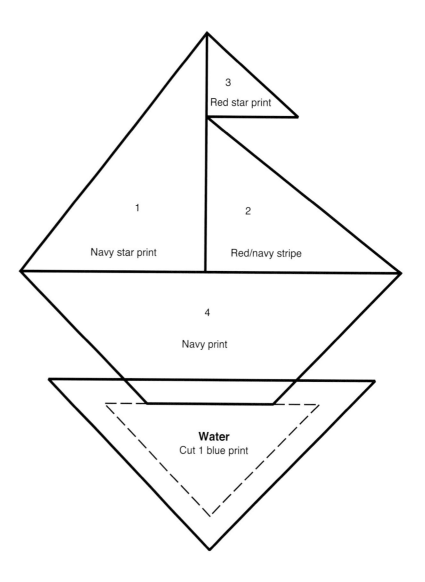

Sunflower Coaster
Placement Diagram
4 1/2" x 4 1/2"

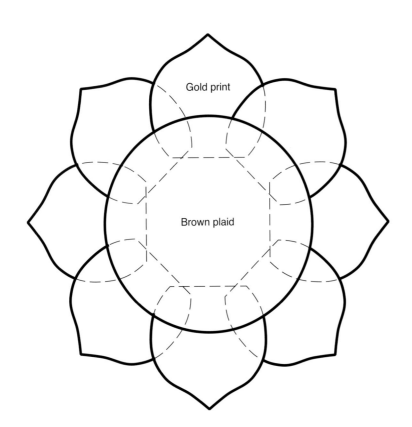

Gold print

Brown plaid

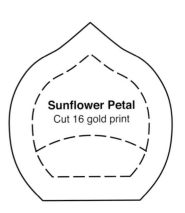

Sunflower Petal
Cut 16 gold print

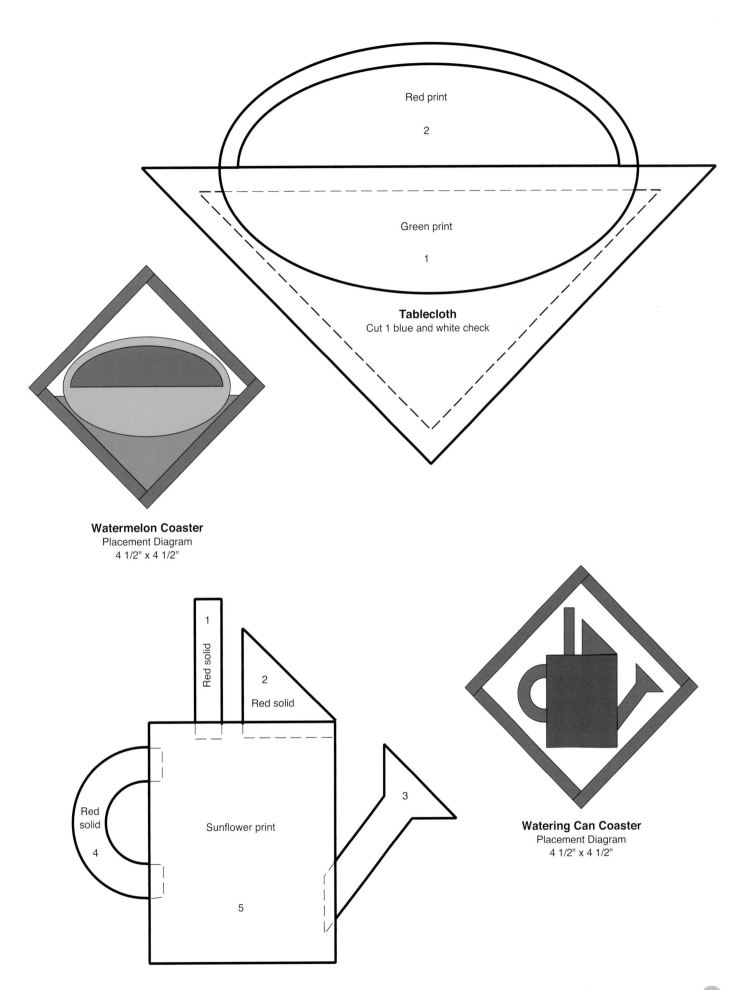

Tablecloth
Cut 1 blue and white check

Red print
2

Green print
1

Watermelon Coaster
Placement Diagram
4 1/2" x 4 1/2"

Watering Can Coaster
Placement Diagram
4 1/2" x 4 1/2"

Red solid
1

Red solid
2

Red solid
4

Sunflower print
5

3

Fall Coaster Set

When we think of fall, seasonal images that come to mind are pumpkins, corn, apples, leaves and more. As the harvest season is in full swing and the leaves begin to change and fall, make this coaster set to include the colors of the season.

Leaf Coaster
Placement Diagram
4 1/2" x 4 1/2"

Project Specifications
Coaster Size: 4½" x 4½"
Block Size: 4" x 4"
Number of Blocks: 4

Materials for the Set
- 10" x 10" square cream solid for background
- Scraps brown/gold, autumn multicolor, light yellow/green, dark yellow/green, olive, green, red, orange and brown prints for appliqué
- Fat quarter fall leaf print for backing and borders
- 10" x 10" square batting
- 10" x 10" piece fusible transfer web
- All-purpose thread to match appliqué fabrics and backing
- Dark green and dark brown all-purpose thread
- Basic sewing supplies and tools

Cutting Chart for the Set
1. Cut four squares cream solid 4½" x 4½" for background.
2. Cut four squares fall leaf print 5" x 5" for backing.
3. Cut four squares batting 5" x 5".
4. Cut eight strips fall leaf print ¾" x 4½" for borders.
5. Cut eight strips fall leaf print ¾" x 5" for borders.

Instructions
1. Follow General Instructions for Machine Appliqué and Special Instructions noted with individual patterns to complete this set.

Apple Special Instructions
1. Stitch stem base line using dark brown thread.

Maple Leaf Special Instructions
1. Stitch leaf veins using dark brown thread.

Pumpkin Special Instructions
1. Stitch tendrils and leaf veins using dark green thread.
2. Stitch pumpkin lines using dark brown thread. ●

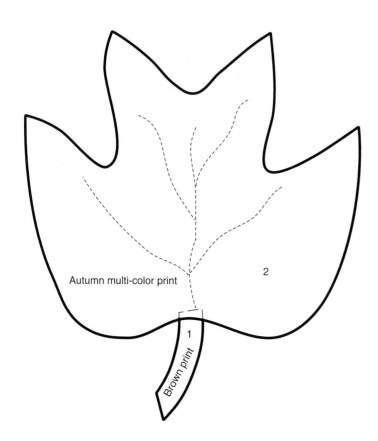

Autumn multi-color print

2

1

Brown print

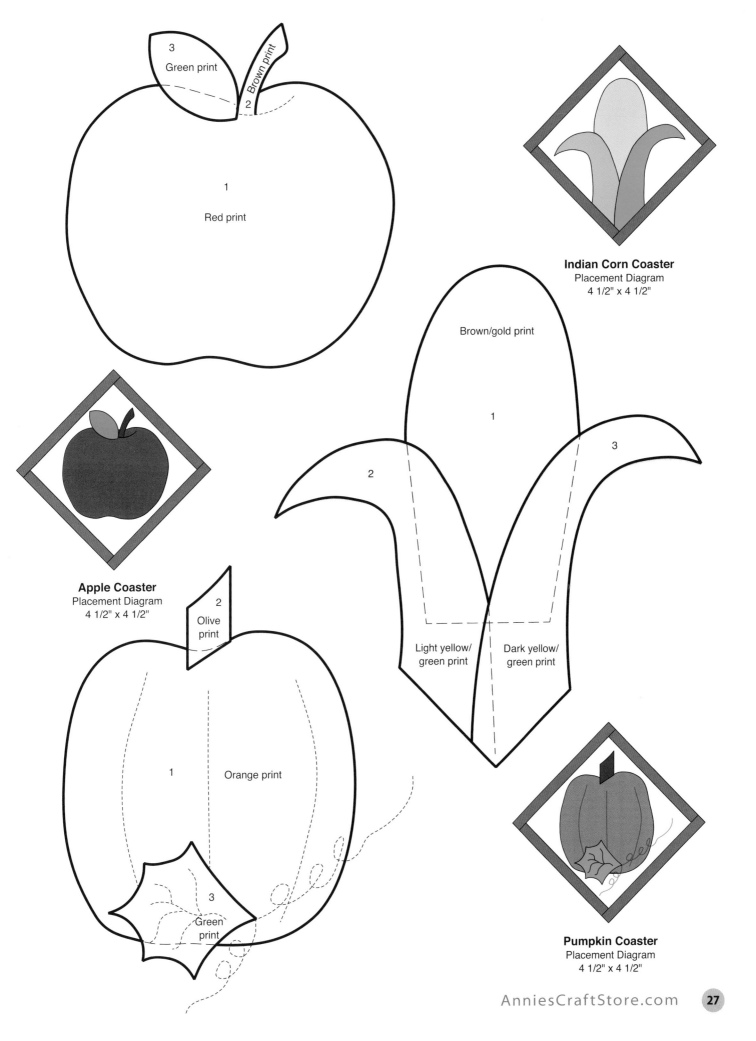

3
Green print

Brown print

2

1
Red print

Indian Corn Coaster
Placement Diagram
4 1/2" x 4 1/2"

Brown/gold print

1

2

3

Apple Coaster
Placement Diagram
4 1/2" x 4 1/2"

Light yellow/
green print

Dark yellow/
green print

2
Olive
print

1   Orange print

3
Green
print

Pumpkin Coaster
Placement Diagram
4 1/2" x 4 1/2"

AnniesCraftStore.com

27

Those Old Animals Coaster Set

Creatures great and small have quilt block designs named for them.
These four patterns are old favorites among quiltmakers.

Project Specifications

Coaster Size: 4½" x 4½"
Block Size: 4" x 4"
Number of Blocks: 4

Materials for the Set

- Fat quarter neutral taupe plaid for background
- Scraps several plaids in assorted colors
- Scraps 6 green plaids
- Scraps 6 blue plaids
- Fat quarter black solid for backing and borders
- 10" x 10" square batting
- 1 spool each cream and black all-purpose thread
- Basic sewing supplies and tools

Cutting Chart for the Set

1. Cut four squares each backing and batting 5" x 5".
2. Cut eight strips black solid ¾" x 4½" for borders.
3. Cut eight strips black solid ¾" x 5" for borders.

Instructions

1. Follow General Instructions for Pieced Coasters to complete this set. ●

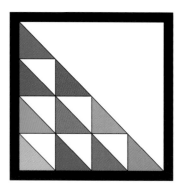

Birds in the Air Coaster
Placement Diagram
4 1/2" x 4 1/2"

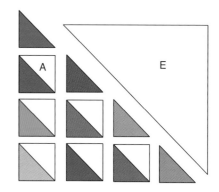

Birds in the Air
Block Piecing Diagram
Lay out pieces to complete 1 Birds in the Air block.

Birds in the Air Units
Join triangles to make units

Birds in the Air Template Cutting Chart

A—Cut 6 background & 10 assorted plaids

E—Cut 1 background

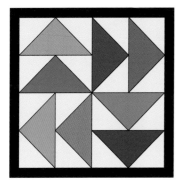

Wild Goose Chase Coaster
Placement Diagram
4 1/2" x 4 1/2"

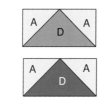

Wild Goose Chase Units
Piece quarters as shown.

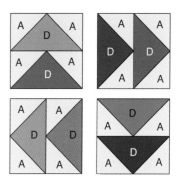

Wild Goose Chase
Block Piecing Diagram
Lay out pieces to complete 1 Wild
Goose Chase block.

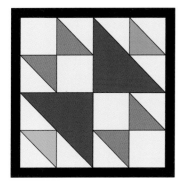

Fox & Geese Coaster
Placement Diagram
4 1/2" x 4 1/2"

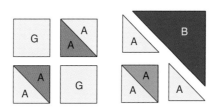

Fox & Geese Units
Piece quarters of block as shown.

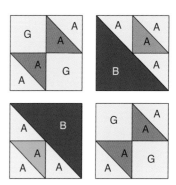

Fox & Geese
Block Piecing Diagram
Lay out pieces to complete 1 Fox & Geese block.

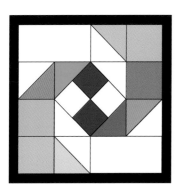

Snail's Trail Coaster
Placement Diagram
4 1/2" x 4 1/2"

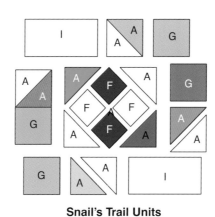

Snail's Trail Units
Piece units, placing green pieces on one
side and blue on other side as shown.

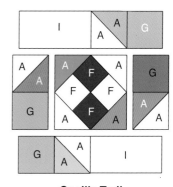

Snail's Trail
Block Piecing Diagram
Join units to complete 1 block.

**Wild Goose Chase
Template Cutting Chart**

A—Cut 16 background

D—Cut 8 assorted plaids

**Fox & Geese Template
Cutting Chart**

A—Cut 6 assorted plaids & 10
background

B—Cut 2 dark plaid

G—Cut 4 background

Snail's Trail Template Cutting Chart

A—Cut 3 each assorted green & blue
plaids & 6 background

F—Cut 1 each green & blue plaids &
2 background

G—Cut 2 each assorted green & blue
plaids

I —Cut 2 background

Full Bloom Coaster Set

Flower shapes detailed with quilting lines make quick and easy coasters.

Project Specifications

Coaster Size: Approximately 4½" x 5"
Block Size: Approximately 4½" x 5"
Number of Blocks: 4

Materials for the Set

- 12" x 12" square each light and dark pink, yellow and lavender mottled solids
- 12" x 12" square batting
- All-purpose thread to match each fabric
- Basic sewing supplies and tools

Instructions

1. Trace the cutting and sewing lines for each flower on the back of the appropriate fabrics.

2. For each flower, place same color pieces right sides together; place batting under and pin. Cut along outside line.

3. Place flower front onto the pattern, right side up; trace the dashed quilting lines onto the flower front, using a light box or if necessary, taping both to a window to see lines.

4. Place flower back onto the pattern, right side up; trace the dashed sewing line onto the flower back.

5. Place flower front and back right sides together with batting under the flower front; pin.

6. Stitch along the sewing line marked on the flower back fabric, leaving a 2" opening on one side. Turn right sides out through opening. Hand-stitch the opening closed with matching thread.

7. Hand- or machine-quilt along the marked quilting lines to finish. ●

Note: *Please photocopy patterns at 175% for full-size patterns*

Pansy Coaster
Placement Diagram
Approximately 4 1/2" x 5"

Rose Coaster
Placement Diagram
Approximately 4 1/2" x 5"

Pansy
Cut 2 lavender
(reverse 1)

Rose
Cut 2 dark pink
(reverse 1)

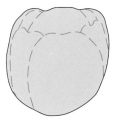

Peony Coaster
Placement Diagram
Approximately 4 1/2" x 5"

Tulip Coaster
Placement Diagram
Approximately 4 1/2" x 5"

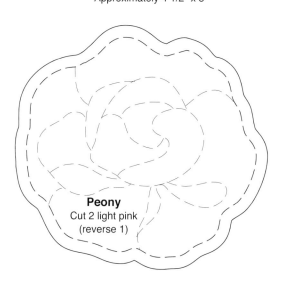

Peony
Cut 2 light pink
(reverse 1)

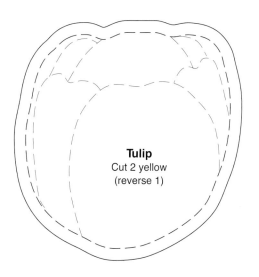

Tulip
Cut 2 yellow
(reverse 1)

RETAIL STORES: If you would like to carry this publication or any other Annie's publication, visit AnniesWSL.com.

Every effort has been made to ensure that the instructions in this publication are complete and accurate. We cannot, however, take responsibility for human error, typographical mistakes or variations in individual work. Please visit AnniesCustomerService.com to check for pattern updates.

ISBN: 978-1-59012-983-8

56789